BUILDING THE LANCASTER CANAL

Written and Illustrated

by

Robert Philpotts

BLACKWATER BOOKS

CONTENTS

Acknowledgements

This book is a revised version of one published by S. Martins College, Lancaster in April 1979. Now, as then, I would like to thank the Principal and Staff and especially Mr. Ben Holgate and the Art Department for their assistance. I would also like to thank Mr. Barry Jones for checking the script.

First published 1979
Revised and reprinted 1983, 1989, 1993, 2000

This edition published 2005
Printed by Japan Cambodia Friendship Printing House
72, 99 Street, Sangkat Phsar Doem Thkov, Khan Chamkarmon,
Phnom Penh, Kingdom of Cambodia

Published by Blackwater Books, 45 Approach Road, London E2 9LY

ISBN 0 946632 00 7

1 Lancaster 1790

Travel in England is quite easy today and if someone wants to go from Preston to Lancaster they have several ways open to them. If they have a car they can simply drive up the motorway or if they prefer to let someone else take them they can catch a bus or go to the railway station and board a train – if they are wealthy they can even hire a taxi! Whichever way they choose it will not take much more than an hour to cover the distance between the two towns. But travel has not always been so simple. In 1790 our Preston to Lancaster traveller would have had no railway train or bus to catch and there were no motor cars. He would have had a choice of transport but we would think all of them to be primitive and uncomfortable.

Mr. Pedder was a founder of a Bank that had been established in Church Street, Preston. As a banker he had to try and maintain contact with important people in his own and surrounding towns. One of the most important people in Lancaster at the time was Abram Rawlinson, a wealthy merchant and it may well have been that Mr. Pedder had occasion to visit Mr. Rawlinson on business matters sometime in 1790. If so he would have had to decide how he was going to travel. He could have gone by sea for both Preston and Lancaster were ports and between the two ships would sail. Mr. Pedder may have asked the captain of such a ship if he could join his vessel for the voyage. In the summer with a gentle, warm breeze and a friendly crew this could be the most pleasant way to make the journey, but if the wind was sharp, the sea rough and the sailors ill tempered then it could be very unpleasant; the traveller having to crouch below deck, feeling gloomy, ill and cold and wondering all the time if the boat would be wrecked.

The only alternative to the sea voyage was to travel by road – but this would have its drawbacks too. In 1790 not a single road in England had the hard, black tarmac surface with which we are familiar today. For the most part roads were rough, earth tracks which after hot and sunny weather became hard and dusty and after rain turned to ribbons of mud. Attempts had been made in the 18th century to improve some of the most important highways in the country (like the one between Preston and Lancaster) by making what was known as a Turnpike or toll road. This meant that gates were erected at either end of a stretch of road and men employed to collect money from road users. This money was then spent on improving the road surface. Although it was a good idea there were all sorts of problems. To begin with stone of the right quality for road building was not always available nearby. In north and north-east Lancashire there was plenty of excellent roadstone but in the southern parts of the county much less than needed and so it had to be brought by ship from Wales or Scotland which was very expensive. Even when the stone actually arrived at the road it was not always used in the best way for although there were some excellent road builders (Thomas Telford was one) working in the country the people employed on Turnpikes did not always follow the best example in either the construction or the repair of the highway. This was most unsatisfactory however for, in Lancashire especially, there was far more traffic using the roads than ever before. After 1750 south Lancashire had become the most industrialised place in the world. England entered a period that we now call the Industrial Revolution and many factories were built in towns such as Colne, Blackburn and Manchester. This put a great strain on the roads in the area for raw materials and finished manufactured goods had to be carried to and from the port of Liverpool and the new factories and more food had to be taken to the towns to feed their growing populations.

Mr. Pedder, stroking his chin in Preston and wondering how to get to Lancaster, would have seen the variety of waggons used for this growing trade. The biggest of all was the stage waggon. Hun-

dreds of these creaked and groaned up and down the country drawn by eight, sometimes ten horses; they carried all sorts of goods beneath their canvas covers and could weigh eight tons when fully loaded. Poor people would travel in the back too sometimes but though it was a cheap way to make a journey it was very slow and could be most uncomfortable. Supplementing the stage waggon were many smaller waggons and carts which were used for local carrying and pack horse teams that were used in areas where the roads were just too bad for wheeled vehicles.

Rather than going as a companion to poor and often smelly and ragged people in a stage waggon. Mr. Pedder would probably decide to either hire a horse or take a ride in a stage coach. If he chose the latter he could, on most mornings, board a fast coach that was due to reach Lancaster by midday. He could opt to go inside or on top. In the colder months if he chose to ride outside he would soon feel the effects of the cutting wind no matter how thick his coat. As the driver urged on his horses the coach body would begin to pitch and sway as the wheels bounced over the rough mending. If the road was very muddy then there might be a sudden diversion as the coachman would swing his team over the verge and across the fields, or, if a single horseman was seen waiting, then an armed passenger might finger his pistol just in case this was a highwayman. All through the journey the passengers would pray that they would not hear a sharp crack above the thunder and rattle of horses and coach for that might mean the parting of wheel and axle and the sudden overturn of the whole machine! But if the vehicle was not subject to any mishaps if it pounded on past lines of packhorses and droves of cattle, splattering pedestrians with mud or choking them with dust then Lancaster would come into view just after eleven and it would bounce down Back Lane and come to a halt at the Royal Oak in Market Place. There it would drop some passengers, and take on more who were bound for Kendal or Carlisle, the steaming horse team might be changed and within a few minutes the coach would be off again clattering down towards the new bridge and the road to the north leaving Mr. Pedder, aching in every bone, to recover in the warming parlour of an inn.

The Lancaster that Mr. Pedder would find would be as busy as Preston. Some 9000 people lived in homes that clustered around the castle. It had a market every Saturday and Wednesday when people from all the surrounding villages would make their way to town to buy what they needed and to sell what they had made, had grown, or had collected from their animals. There was usually a good supply of grain, oat meal, fruit, vegetables, butter, poultry and eggs for sale on the open stalls, fish was cheap and plentiful from both the Lune and Morecambe Bay and three times a year there were extra large markets specially organised for the sale of cattle, cheese and cloth. But the market alone had not made Lancaster the thriving place that it was in 1790 nor created the wealth necessary to pay for much of the new building that had taken place or was planned for the future. This extra money came from Lancaster's ships and especially from the trade they carried on with Africa and the West Indies. Lancaster, though no where near the size of Bristol or London or Liverpool had more ships engaged in the West India trade than all (apart from these three) the other ports of England together.

If Mr. Pedder had had to wait an hour or so he might have left the Inn and set off to wander the town. In the centre he would have found a fine new Town Hall which had been completed in 1783. For the amusement of the most prosperous Lancastrians an assembly room nearby had winter concerts at which men of the Musical Society would perform and a theatre had been built in 1781 which was hired out to companies of travelling players. But

the more well-to-do did not spend all of their time in pleasure for there was much charitable work done in the town too. A new Poor House had recently been built on the edge of Lancaster Moor, there were alms houses like Penny's Hospital for poor old people and for some of the poor young there were Boys and Girls Charitable Schools. Near the Castle a Dispensary had been established in 1785 to provide for the needs of the sick and this had a good number of patients – too many perhaps. Certainly the number could have been reduced if the citizens of Lancaster had spent as much on building below ground as above. In 1790 there were no proper sewers in the town and rubbish was dumped in the middle of the streets to be carried, when rain swept in from the sea,

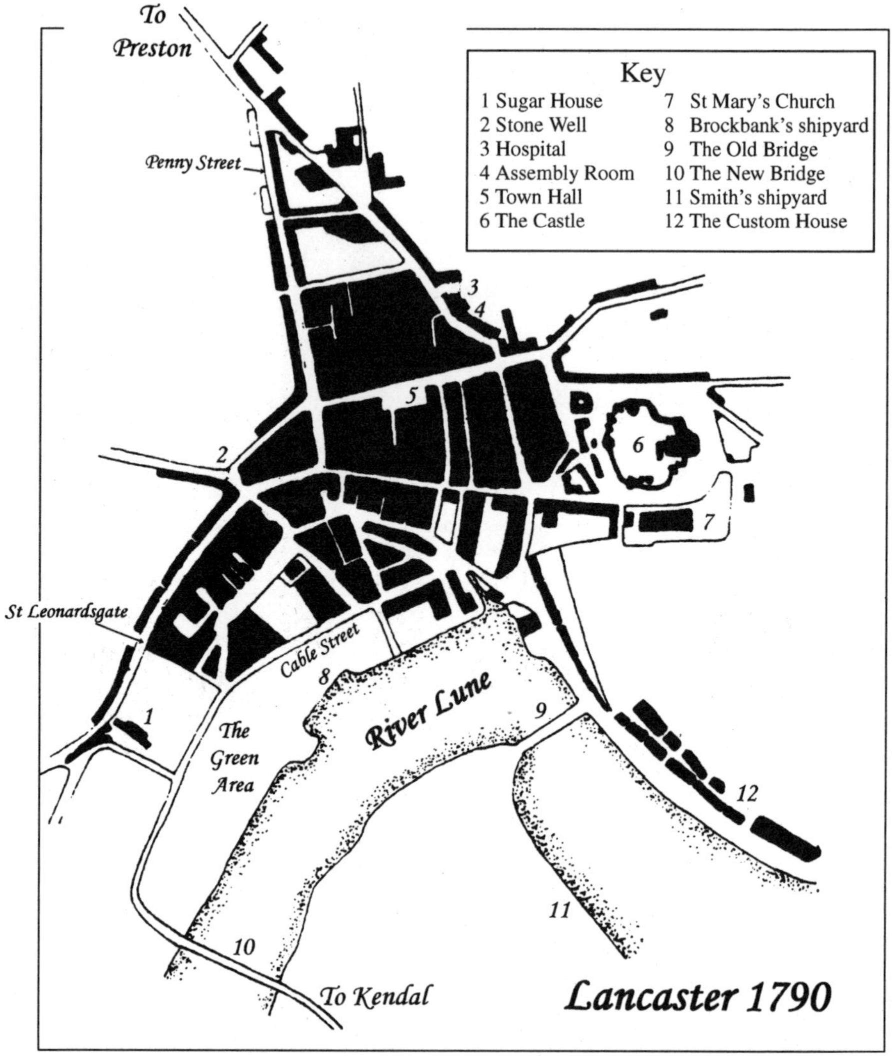

down to the two huge gratings at the Stone Well from where it was floated away by a little natural stream to the river. In hot summer months especially poor sanitation must have been the cause of much illness.

If Mr. Pedder had walked down to the Stone Well and then

along St. Leonardsgate he would soon have come to the Sugar House. Beyond were only a few houses before open country began. so our traveller may have started back along the busy riverside. At the Green Area he would have found shipbuilding in progress and further along Cable Street would have seen the impressive, newly built and mahogany doored houses bought by men who were making their money, these contrasting with the small, tightly packed and sometimes thatched cottages and houses in which most of the families of Lancaster lived. Walking along Dam Side into Bridge Lane he would pass the crumbling old Lune Bridge before finally arriving at St. Georges Quay. Here he would see boats being loaded and unloaded under the suspicious eye of the Customs man who had an office set amongst the warehouses. Working on the quay would be sailors and dockworkers and, standing apart, groups of merchants and boat owners discussing quality, prices and profits. If Mr. Pedder had joined them in conversation then he would soon have heard of their worries and plans and of how they felt their trade threatened by the growing size and importance of Liverpool. Lancaster was not a particularly good natural port because of the shifting sands of the Lune estuary. Five miles downstream however, builders working under the direction of the Lancaster Port Commissioners had recently completed what was believed to be the finest dock in England capable of holding 25 merchant ships. But the Glasson Dock facilities were attractive only to seamen, when a cargo was unloaded it still had to be taken by pack horse, cart or waggon across country and Mr. Pedder himself knew how difficult that could be. For many years there had been an idea around that Lancaster could be connected to the south by building a canal, but they came to nothing although other canals built around Liverpool had certainly helped that port. Now however from all over the country came talk of new canals being planned and the merchants must have wondered if the time was right to try again.

Since Abram Rawlinson was one of the most important merchants in the town then it may well have been that the conversation turned to canals when Mr. Pedder finally kept his appointment. Mr. Rawlinson was a wealthy man who lived in a house that he insured for £1000 (a great deal of money in 1790) and had half a dozen servants and two carriages. When Britain was at war with someone or other, which was quite often, ships would set out from Lancaster and other ports to raid enemy shipping. They were not part of the Navy but they were not pirates either. Instead they were called Privateers. Abram had shares in Privateering and as a result handled booty such as Mexican silver coins. He liked to gamble, buying lottery tickets quite regularly but was also a religious man, renting a pew at St. Mary's Church by the year. He subscribed to both the Charity Schools and the Dispensary and was generous with his servants and family.

Now Abram Rawlinson would have had the same concerns as the merchants on the dock but, being a man fond of his home and being sympathetic to those in less fortunate circumstances than himself he knew what a difference a canal would make in ordinary houses in Lancaster and its surrounding villages. In the climate of north Lancashire, warmth in the cold and damp months was of great concern, but fuel was scarce and expensive. Coal was usually brought by coaster from the Wigan area via the River Douglas and Ribble estuary. Once at Lancaster however it had to be transported by waggon and this was costly. Although Mr. Rawlinson made the bulk of his wealth from trade, he did have some interest in agriculture too and though not a great landowner, knew how important a canal could be to farmers. One of the best fertilizers that they had was made from limestone. This was dug from quarries and then burnt either in kilns nearby or near the fields on which it was to be used. Although the local limestone beds were all in the north of Lancashire, farmers around Lancaster found it cost them a good deal to transport and it was even more expensive to take further south.

So Mr. Rawlinson and Mr. Pedder must have agreed on how valuable a canal built between the limestone beds in the north and the coal fields of the south would be. Not only would a cheap form of transport benefit farmers and merchants, everybody from the largest landowner to the poor labourer looking glumly at his empty grate would find his life improved by such a new canal.

2 Plans

When an engineer named John Longbotham suggested in 1772 that a canal be built to link Liverpool with Leeds money poured in to support his scheme. Some influential Lancaster men, not wishing that their town be left out of things had an engineer named Robert Whitworth draw up a plan to build a waterway that would run from Kendal through Lancaster and down to south Lancashire. But though work on the Leeds and Liverpool got started, on the Lancaster it did not – at least not for another twenty years.

By 1791 however Lancaster men could see just how beneficial the canals that had been recently dug in England had been to the towns they served. That was why twenty-nine men who had influence, money and power and the most to gain from the building of a canal came together and composed a letter to the Mayor of Lancaster. They said . . . .

"The advantage the town of Liverpool has derived from inland navigations . . . has given . . . . the merchants and traders in that place so decided a superiority in the vend of their imports as greatly to diminish the commerce of this town . . . . It appears to the Persons subscribing this letter that the sole and most profitable method of . . . competing with Liverpool . . . . is by a canal from this town or its vicinity to join the from Liverpool to Leeds

Mayor Atkinson agreed and called a meeting and so it was that at 10 o'clock in the morning of June 8th, 1791 men from

Lancashire and Westmorland and even further afield made their way through the rough paved streets to the Town Hall of Lancaster. It must be remembered that probably all of the people who came to the meeting were men, for few women played an active part in matters of this kind in those days – their place was in the home. The great majority of male wage earners were excluded too for very few of them could afford to take time off work for a meeting like this. They had to trust that the wealthier citizens of their town would do what was best for all. But even with so many people left out the meeting would have seen a mixed bag of characters. Old men with sticks and ear trumpets, young legal men with long fingers and clean nails, farmers in twenty year old coats and merchants with clothes that had an aroma of spice. The gathering would quieten as one of the group of canal advocates stood up and began to speak. It may have been John Brockbank the shipbuilder or Thomas Rawlinson, a relation of Abram but whoever it was the message would have been the same – a canal was vital to the future of Lancaster. To get one built extensive preparations were necessary and the stages of this preparation would have been outlined.

They were . . . .

Stage 1 Opinion about the canal had to be taken from the landowners through whose land the canal would pass. This was especially important as far as the biggest landlords were concerned for if just one of these was awkward, then he could make all sorts of difficulties for the canal planners.

Stage 2 Some definite idea of where the canal should run had to be drawn up. The route of a canal was known as the line and the line would be drawn up by a surveyor or an engineer. He had to be paid for his work and so stage 2 ran along with . . .

Stage 3 Collecting money. This was a vital task. When a new transport system is built today most of the money comes from the Government or local authority but this was not the case in the C18th. The success or failure of a canal project depended upon having sufficient money to pay for each stage of its planning and construction

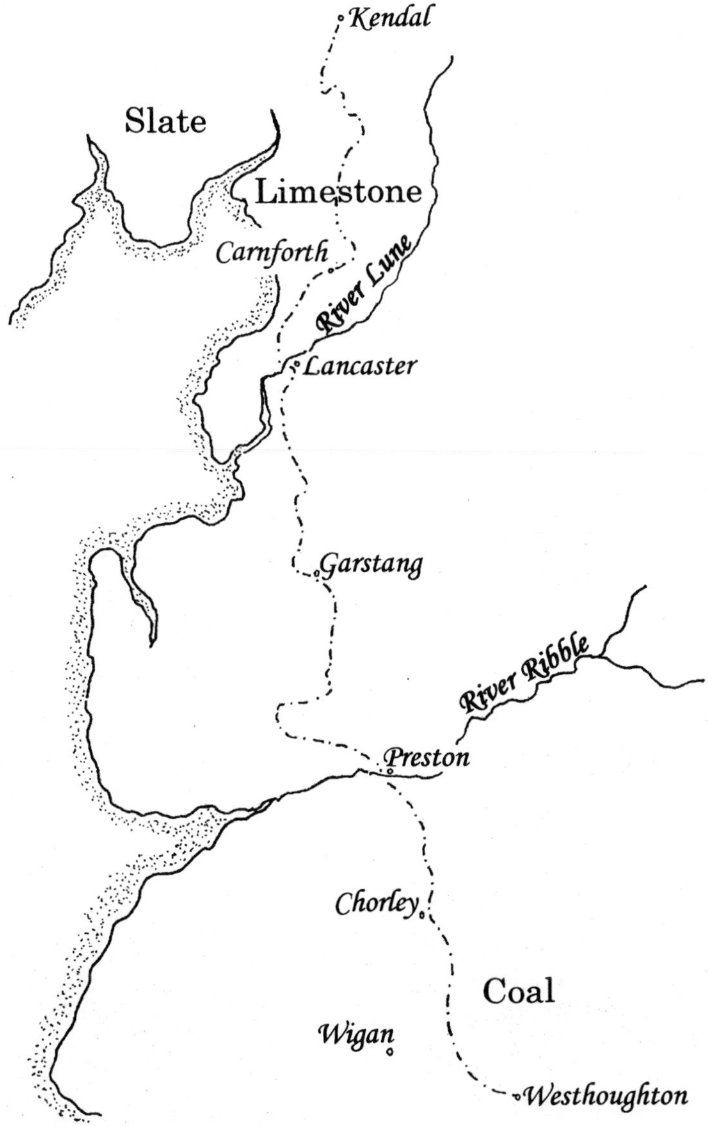

Sketch map of John Rennie's line of 1792

and this money had to come from voluntary subscription.

Stage 4 When a line had been drawn up then an Act of Parliament had to be passed to allow a company to be set up which could then force landowners to sell the land needed for the construction of the canal. If there was any opposition to the canal however then Parliament might refuse to pass an act and all the money that had been spent and all the planning that had been done would be wasted. Therefore it was important that as much support as possible in the form of petitions were got together before the matter was debated in Parliament.

When the spokesman had finished his outline it was time to decide on the places between which the canal would run and to elect a committee to organise the plans for getting an Act. It was decided that Kendal was the best place for a northern terminal. This town was an important market centre and was supplied with coal from the same source as Lancaster and as it also had easy access to slate quarries it was believed that the extra cost of building a Lancaster to Kendal waterway would be justified by a good traffic in coal, limestone and slate. What would happen at the other end of the canal was less sure though it was hoped that some connection would be made with other canals, perhaps with the Bridgewater or the Leeds and Liverpool. And so the meeting broke up and the word was passed around the town that the Lancaster Canal was going ahead – though some old men must have grinned, shaken their heads and mumbled that they had heard it all before.

During the next six weeks an agent of the Committee made his way around Lancashire to find out the opinions of those men of property through whose land the canal might run. On the whole he found they supported the idea. At the same time subscription books were opened in Blackburn, Manchester, Bolton, Liverpool, Settle, Kendal, Preston, Chorley, London and Garstang so that people could contribute to the cost of making the survey and the other expenses which were being incurred. Samuel Gregson was employed as Clerk to the Committee at a yearly salary of £150 and was allowed ten shillings and sixpence (52½p) a day for horse hire and travelling expenses if he had to go away from Lancaster on

committee business. He rented a small office at the Judges Lodgings near the Castle for five shillings (25p) a week and for this his landlord also agreed to provide a fire.

In order to work out an exact line that could be presented to Parliament the Committee decided to approach John Rennie to make a survey and estimate of the cost of building the Lancaster Canal. Rennie was a Scotsman who had been a millwright before becoming an expert in mechanical engineering and making a reputation in planning public works. He had connections with other canal schemes, the committee found him cheaper to employ than John Longbotham and it took him no more than two months to make his survey of a canal that was to be almost 76 miles in length.

There were to be 41 locks altogether and two great aqueducts. The two main level sections were to be between Westhoughton and Clayton Green (15½ miles) and Tewitfield and Preston (42½ miles). The committee were pleased with Rennie's work and before his plan had even been presented for general public approval resolved that petitions from the principal towns of Lancashire and

Westmorland be obtained so that they could be sent to Parliament in time for the presentation of the Lancaster Canal Act.

On February 7th another public meeting was called in the Town Hall and it was found that midwinter had not withered the enthusiaasm of summer. So great in fact was the confidence of the meeting that nearly a quarter of a million pounds was subscribed towards the cost of getting the Act and the building work itself. Rennie's line was adopted and the Committee was urged to press ahead. Enthusiasm and money were not always enough to influence Parliament however and the committee knew that there would be those who would oppose their scheme for one reason or another. Because of this they decided to send a special party to London in order that they might push through their canal act at the first attempt. At the end of February therefore Abram Rawlinson and a handful of others packed their bags, kissed their families goodbye and set off to the capital.

Even if they had visited the city before the London of 1792 would have seemed a bewildering, bustling place to the north countryman. Compared with Lancaster it was huge, its streets thronged with all manner of beggars and sellers as well as the most

elegant and fashionable of women and the wealthiest and most dashing of young men.

Although there were many carriages for hire, a pleasant afternoon on the river would give the best panorama of the city. Dominating everything was St. Paul's Cathedral, although many other church spires pointed skywards above the tiled roofs and other attractive buildings stood by the riverfront. One of these was the Houses of Parliament and it was here that the future of the Lancaster Canal Act was to be decided. It was necessary for those with a Canal Bill to have the support of at least one important and influential member of Parliament and it was fortunate for the Lancaster party that not only the Earl of Balcarees but also the Duke of Bridgewater (one of the men who had begun recent canal development in England) supported their scheme. None the less they did meet with objections and were forced to alter their Act accordingly. The question of water supply for example gave cause for concern for a good many people. The Lancaster Canal supporters wanted to use the River Mint to feed their canal but a number of mill and factory owners objected because they thought that this might take the water that they needed to drive their water wheels. Safeguards were therefore written into the Act to ensure that the needs of the mills and factories would be put before those of the canal in times of water shortage. Rennie had also suggested that water might be pumped by steam engine from other rivers and streams that ran by the line of the canal but because of objections many of these were denied to the canal company. Mr. William Bradshaw Bradshaw of Lancaster objected that if water was taken from the Lune or if an aqueduct was built it would disturb the fishing that he did at Skerton in water held by specially constructed weirs. Safeguards were therefore put in the Act to protect him too.

Almost until the day the Bill was presented to Parliament discussion also took place between the London Party and the Lancaster Committee as to just how much would be charged for goods carried on the canal. Money was raised by tollage in a similar way to that on a turnpike road. If a boat was carrying coal for instance it would be charged a certain fee or toll based on the amount carried and the distance it was taken. It was finally decided that the toll for coal over most of the canal was to be one and a half pence (about ½p) per ton per mile.

Apart from problems with water and tollage arguments arose with landowners who were jealous over the use of their property for the making of a canal. To keep them happy a number of concessions were made. They were to be allowed to fish in the canal and to carry their animals on it free of charge within the limits of their own estates. One landowner was even given permission to build, if he ever so wished his own branch to carry goods from the Lancaster Canal into his own estate.

In the end, all this chopping and changing proved to be worthwhile for Abram Rawlinson's party saw the Bill pass the House of Commons and the House of Lords and finally when King George III gave his signature to it on June 11th 1792 it became law. There must have been jubilation in the little northern town as the news reached home and Abram no doubt celebrated in style.

3 Getting started

With the Act passed the first thing that the committee did was to organise itself properly. A new committee of 11 men (9 from Lancaster and one each from Kendal and Preston) was elected. All of the members had been actively involved in getting the Act including John Brockbank. Strangely Abram Rawlinson never joined the committee himself but Thomas Rawlinson no doubt safeguarded his interests.

It was the job of the committee to see that the canal was built and it was directly responsible to the people who were to pay for this. Many people wanted to subscribe to the canal building and the Act allowed for shares to be sold at £100 each. In charge of selling these shares and of handling the companies finances generally was the treasurer and the committee appointed Mr. Thomas Worswick to the position. He had to give a bond of £20,000 so he must have been a wealthy man or have had wealthy friends. The clerk to the committee was just as important as the treasurer, for he had to ensure that the instructions of the committee were carried out. Samuel Gregson was a natural choice for this position and so was appointed.

With the administration organised, the committee set about preparing for the actual building of the canal. As their chief agent they employed John Rennie. He was to be the Principal Engineer and was to design all the major features of the canal including the aqueduct over the Lune. Since Rennie did not intend to be on the line during all the time of the construction however, the committee looked around for a competent engineer to fill the post of Resident Engineer. He had to be "a person capable of conducting the business of the canal . . . . a good engineer" with a perfect knowledge of cutting, banking and . . . a complete mason". There were to be two employed – one for the canal section to be built north of the Ribble and the other for that to be built to the south. Eventually they agreed to employ a Mr. Archibald Millar who had previously worked as an agent on the Clyde Navigation in Scotland and a Mr. Henry Eastburn who had recently been employed on the Basingstoke Canal. Along with these engineers the committee decided to employ supervisors to make sure that the cutting of the canal was done properly and that the wood and stone work was of a good standard. Although the Principal Engineer, the Resident Engineer and the lesser supervisors were to be paid by the company, the committee decided that it would be best to leave the actual construction of the canal to big contractors who had experience with this kind of work before. As it turned out their decision was the wrong one, but the committee were not to know that at the time. And so as the search for good supervisors was going on adverts were appearing in newspapers published as far apart as Edinburgh and London saying that the building of the first stage of the canal would be let to contract. This meant that building contractors were invited to give a price for their work in constructing a particular section of the canal. The committee would then look at all the different prices (or tenders) and decide who should be given the contract to do it. Generally they gave it to the man or men who gave the lowest price and who seemed to be the most reliable. It had been decided that the line would be divided into four sections

Section 1 *Between Borwick and Ellel Grange*
Section 2 *Between Ellel Grange and Hollowforth Bridge*
Section 3 *Between Hollowforth Bridge and the River Ribble*
Section 4 *Between the River Ribble and West Houghton*

Although the Lune Aqueduct was to be built it was decided that work on the Borwick to Kendal section of the canal and the aqueduct over the River Ribble would not, due to cost, be proceeded with until it was seen how the work in general was going.

By the end of December 1792 several contractors had given in their estimates for stage one and it was decided to give the contract

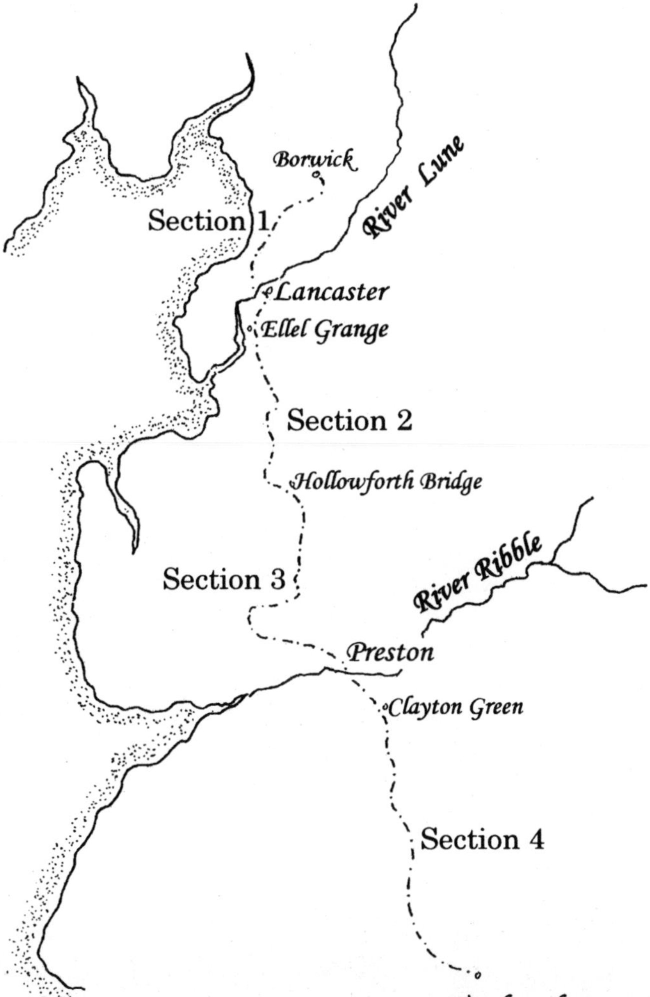

The four sections

to John Pinkerton and John Murray on the basis of their price of £52,000. The Lune Aqueduct was let separately however – to a Scots contractor named Alexander Stevens.

Once Pinkerton and Murray had the contract they were quick off the mark in getting started. Since they were well known contractors and were working on other canals at the same time they had no difficulty in getting men to come and work for them. So to Lancaster came the diggers (or cutters as they were sometimes known). They trudged tens, sometimes hundreds of miles to get there, occasionally cadging lifts on waggons, but more often than not ending the day footsore.

Experienced men on the tramp might carry a spare set of clothes, a few belongings and a shovel with a polished blade and shaft worn smooth in use, others might have nothing but a few pence and a pocketful of breadcrumbs. Some walked from Scotland, coming through Kendal and Carlisle in the biting January wind, others came from Ireland by cargo boat. But in the main the men who were to work on the Lancaster Canal were Englishmen. Some were southerners who had left the mellowness of the Thames valley or the Cotswolds to walk through the Midlands to see the rugged north country for the first time, but the majority were from the towns and villages of Lancashire and Yorkshire, Westmorland and Cumberland. When the travelling cutters and others finally arrived on the line, they would have to find lodgings. If they were working in Lancaster or near a sizeable village like Carnforth this would be

relatively easy, but out in the country much more difficult. In that case a farmyard outbuilding might be rented as a temporary lodging house. When a very large group of men were to be concentrated in one spot then the company might help out – at the Lune Aqueduct for instance lodging rooms were built for the workmen by the riverside.

The day of the digger or navigator (navvy as he became known) started early. Since most men would sleep in most of their clothes under a dirty woollen blanket they would have to pull on only their old boots and patched top coat to be ready for work. A swill in an icy stream or a wooden tub and a breakfast of cold beer, bread and gritty porridge and they would be off through the frosty dawn down to the works where they would collect their tools for the day. Some men had their own spades to make their work easier, but most would collect a spade, a shovel, a pick or a barrow and set off in the half light to their place of work. By the time it was full day light they would already be setting a steady pace under the eye of a contractors gangerman. The men would work in small groups alternating their jobs, now picking, now shovelling, now barrowing. On a stretch of line they would start by digging a hole and then when it was deep enough start to widen it along the line laid down by the surveyor. Gradually the wide hole would become a trench and then, when joined with the others there would be the appearance of a canal under construction. The earth that was thrown up would be carted off to where a large embankment was being built and to where much extra earth was needed. If a very deep cutting was made then runs may have been constructed and the navvy would spend his day being hauled up a muddy wooden plank to tip his wheelbarrow full of earth into a waggon. Whatever his job the digger would spend all day at it pausing probably only for a lunch of bread, cheese and beer and sheltering, if shelter was to be had only from the worst of the rain and snow. Even after daylight had faded he might work on beneath the glare of a burning bonfire.

Then at the end of his ten hour day and only provided no overtime was required would he be free to return to his sleeping place. With his companions he may have clubbed together to employ a village woman to prepare a meal for their return – a good stew if they were lucky. For the rest of the day the navvies might go to an inn to drink away the aches of the day or, if they were too far out in the country their beer would be swilled in the flickering fire-light as stories were told and retold by any who had come from distant places or who had seen service in the British Forces or the merchant marine.

The gruelling work round continued for six days of the week for as long as the contract continued. The average labouring man could expect to earn two shillings and two pence (11p) per day in April of 1794 and a stonemason three shillings (15p). This was not much even in the 1790's. If conditions were so bad then why did they stay? The answer is that conditions elsewhere were as bad if not worse. At a time when little children of five or six were forced to work sixteen hours a day in cotton mills and when the unemployment of a breadwinner could mean near starvation for a whole family, then the canal worker might have thought himself lucky in many respects, out in the open, knowing the pressures to get the canal completed gave him reasonable security if he worked hard and feeling free of the awful drudgery of the factory or mill.

Although work was started on line around Lancaster in January of 1793 – Gregson reporting that 'We are going very briskly, the cutters and labourers crowd in' the committee still had a great deal of work to do in order that the contractors could keep working at a steady pace. Although a line of the canal had been fixed with the Act of 1792 the company were allowed to deviate by up to 100 yards from it along most of its length. This allowed the waterway to follow the contours of the land closely so reducing the work needed in construction. The exact route of the canal was only really decided when a company engineer was on the spot. As this line survey was going on an agent of the company would contact the owner of the land over which it would pass and try to negotiate a fair price for the needed property. In general a fair price was soon agreed on but sometimes the landowner could be very awkward and refuse to agree on a price or even sell his land at all. When that happened the committee had to go to arbitration. That meant that they had to get other people to decide just what a fair price was. Sometimes more than land was involved. Old barns, cowsheds, even houses could be in the way of the intended cut and then the company would have to purchase them too and knock them down – trying to recoup some of the money spent by selling the materials from which the buildings had been constructed. The slate and timber of an old house that stood by Moor Lane Bridge in Lancaster was sold for six pounds ten shillings (£6.50). Sometimes if a landowner was willing to sell his land but not his buildings then the company got the land, but in turn dismantled obstructing buildings and erected them elsewhere.

Once land had been cleared for construction and when the committee gave permission, the contractor could move his men on the line. The whole of the digging work force did not just start at one point and work outwards from it however. Because of landowner problems and the need to make sure that men always had work to do, digging groups would be stretched out for miles. The cutters would begin digging along a certain section making a trench about 20' wide and 7' deep. When this was done then the bottom and sides had to be made watertight by a process known as puddling. Puddling comprised of filling the bottom and sides of the canal with a waterproof lining of clay and this could vary in thickness according to the type of subsoil. Sometimes it was a yard deep.

CROSS SECTION OF THE CANAL
(Not to Scale)

The towpath was covered with small stones and inclined towards the canal.

The clay had to be treaded to make it impervious to water and one method of doing this was to have navvies stamp up and down on it in their bare feet until all the air bubbles were driven out. Sometimes cattle were driven into the canal bed however and with whoops and yells the navvies would chase them up and down until the clay had been properly puddled.

As the canal was being puddled then the towpath would be prepared. On the Lancaster this was made to incline inwards – possibly to shed water into the canal. Unfortunately should a horse stumble it was more likely to fall into the canal from such a camber and in later years the towpath incline was altered over most of the canal so it inclined the other way, i.e. away from the canal. A covering of small stones or grit would be spread on the towpath when completed to give the barge horses a good footing in their labours.

With puddle and towpath complete the works were tidied up, grass seed was spread over the bare patches or earth and in some places trees were planted. These were usually beech because it was thought their roots were not so likely to spread over long distances and become a danger to the canal itself. The wind and weather would of course tend to wear away the canal banks and the committee were prepared to attend to this in their allowance for regular maintenance, what they were not so prepared for were attacks on the banks by little animals. However a Mr. Richard Robinson came to their assistance for he wrote:

Gentlemen,
As we have been much employed in catching moles in the neighbourhood and we hope much to the satisfaction of our employer and being informed that you want the moles in the banks of your canal catched, we hereby beg leave to offer ourselves to the committee to undertake catching the same.

Whilst the diggers were cutting sections of the line the stonemasons would be erecting accommodation bridges. These were to carry roads or farm tracks over the canal. Where there was an established public right of way this was straight forward. A temporary track would be made around the building site whilst the old road was dug up and a stone bridge erected. When completed the temporary track would be closed and traffic set to run over the new bridge. In the case of farm tracks matters would be more complicated since farmers could be awkward about just where they wanted their bridges built. The company did not want to spend more money than was necessary and would offer to build cheap wooden swivel bridges for tracks that were little used but needed to take animals and vehicles from one part of a farm to another. Some farmers were very difficult about this however and stood on their rights. At Ellers near Milnthorpe there are two excellent stone bridges built within 50 yards of each other. It seems unlikely that the combined amount of traffic they would carry would justify the high cost of their construction and one, no doubt, was built as a result of a farmer's objections to a swivel bridge or his unwillingness to use one that carried a common road.

The material used for building accommodation bridges and culverts and aqueducts was stone. There were many rock outcrops along the length of the line that had been worked for generations for wall, farm and house building and so there was no difficulty in getting raw material, although wood was more of a problem for the construction of swivel bridges and footbridges.

By the spring of 1793 shareholders of the Lancaster Canal Company might, looking at the works from a distance, have been well pleased with the speed at which construction had begun. Unfortunately however there were already undercurrents of trouble and it did not take long for these to surface.

4 Problems

Although their work was straight forward, the line well laid and the materials to hand, the company soon became uneasy about the efforts that Pinkerton and Murray were making to get the canal built properly. Part of the problem was that, in the early months of construction, the company had few proper supervisors on site. The contractors were little better organised and tended to sub-contract. This meant that they adopted the same principle as the company; they would let small lots of work to men who offered the lowest tender. Thus a couple of stonemasons might agree with Pinkerton and Murray to build a bridge for a certain price and then be left to get on with it. Pinkerton and Murray were not always choosy about who they let the contracts to however, for they wanted to get the work completed for the lowest amount possible so that they could make the biggest profit. The consequence of this was often bad work about which the company soon complained and which then caused a great deal of argument. Even when Pinkerton and Murray supervised the work themselves it could leave a great deal to be desired, for they tended to try to 'get away with' as much as possible. Indeed, had it not been for the arrival of the northern section resident engineer, they might have driven the company to near bankrupcy and left the committee with a waterless and unuseable ditch.

Archibald Millar arrived in Lancaster in March of 1793 and was dismayed by what he saw of the canal that had already been built.

He was a tough character who paid at the rate of £400 per year saw his first responsibility as being to the company and therefore of getting the canal built properly. He had little interest in what people said about him, was incorruptable and came into conflict with Pinkerton and Murray almost as soon as he arrived.

Some of the canal had already been filled with water so that boats could be used to move materials from one area to another. This was done by temporarily diverting stream or spring water into a completed section of the canal made water tight by the erection of wooden dams at each end. Once in use it was obviously not possible to check the state of the canal bed unless the water was drained, but Millar was anxious to inspect the puddle as he suspected that it had not been made properly. When he approached Pinkerton and Murray however, they implied that he should mind his own business and called him a 'damned ill natured fellow' when he persisted in his investigations. Millar therefore went to the committee and asked that they support him against the contractors. The committee, fed up with Pinkerton and Murray's slowness in getting the work around Lancaster completed obliged but the enmity between Pinkerton and Murray and Millar remained. The resident engineer found that his instructions were forgotten as soon as his back was turned and that sometimes the canal was being dug yards from the line which he had laid. Exasperated, Millar went to the committee for more assistance and pointed out that if things continued in this way the whole works would be reduced to chaos. He suggested that if Pinkerton and Murray did not do as they were told their payment should be stopped, and even went so far as to urge that the work should be taken from them and given to lots of smaller contractors who would be easier to deal with. The committee were reluctant to do this however, indeed they gave Pinkerton and Murray part of another section of the canal to complete, but Samual Gregson, the clerk to the committee, was determined to give Millar all the help that he wanted.

Normally Millar gave instructions on the conduct of the works to Pinkerton and Murray who then instructed their own workers on what should be done. Pinkerton therefore objected when Millar took to ordering about the workmen himself, but Gregson retorted that the contractors had almost no supervisors on the line and that those that were hardly seemed to know what was going on.

Throughout 1794 the cross fire continued and complaints about Pinkerton and Murray reached Gregson from many quarters. There was trouble over stone. Lack of proper supervision in the quarries meant that the quarrymen, who were quite well paid and who did not want to be out of work during the winter, took their time in cutting the stone. Sometimes therefore there was not enough building material on the line for the work in hand. Often when the stone was being transported from the quarry to the line careless loading meant that rock tumbled from the carts onto the road and it was left there, an obstruction to other traffic. Once, despite Rennie's stipulations Millar caught Pinkerton's men using very soft stone on the Conder aqueduct. There were problems on the line too. When road bridges were started no proper side tracks were made and so the public had to find their own way through adjacent fields and although the contractors were supposed to keep their workmen within a reasonable distance of the canal so as not to unnecessarily damage farm crops, Gregson had to write:

"there are no fences and the gates are all broke – the land is open to the public and is very much trodden and abused".

The clerk was also irritated at the way in which Pinkerton and Murray allowed their men to wander on to land which had not yet been bought by the company, for if a landowner was being difficult such action could upset delicate negotiations. One such landowner was Lord Hamilton of Ashton Hall who had firmly insisted that no water be used from streams that ran through his estate. It was in near panic then that Gregson wrote to the contractors.

"The clamour is raging that you are to have Barrow Beck running into the canal this day – in point blank contradiction to the Act of Parliament – for good Gods sake do not be so very crazy as to turn the said without having full liberty from Lord A. Hamilton."

Money was another bone of contention. When work had been completed it was 'measured'. An agent of the company would work out how much a contractor should be paid according to the amount of earth that had been moved or how many stones laid. There was not always agreement about the figures though and often disagreement developed over just how much work had been done and had to be paid for. On one occasion Pinkerton and Murray said the company owed them £8000 although company records showed that in fact £180 had been overpaid already. Eventually Mr. Worswick paid out £1,500 to keep work moving.

Relations between the company and contractors might have been somewhat better if the work had gone along more quickly and if Pinkerton and Murray had been more reasonable characters. But too often they were galloping away to other canals where they had other work in progress and if Murray was a liar Pinkerton was a know all. When Millar insisted on Pinkerton making a sound 3 foot puddle on part of the line the contractor sneered that there was not another engineer in the country who would think it necessary.

After all of this trouble and when Pinkerton and Murray repeatedly disobeyed Millar's instructions the company decided to rid themselves of the pair. In early 1795 therefore Gregson met them and agreed that their work should be measured up, that they should be paid for it and that then they would go. Millar's suggestion of letting the rest of the work off in small lots was taken up and he met groups of men dismissed by Pinkerton and Murray at the termination of their contract and then employed them as small contractors. Soon there were no less than 35 contractors spread out on the line between Borwick and Preston, all having little contracts of perhaps a couple of bridges or 500 yards of cutting each. Millar found this a great advantage for if he found bad workmanship he could quickly tell the workmen to get off the line and employ someone else to finish the work. For Gregson and Mr. Worwick it meant more work though, for instead of paying one contractor they now had to deal with a large number and it must have been something of a headache for them to keep track. On the whole however Gregson seemed satisfied with the turn of events for in January 1796 he wrote that the 'Good effects of small contracts are visible' and that much of the northern section of the canal was complete.

On the southern section of the canal there was less of a problem with the contractors. The bulk of the cutting work went to a steady Yorkshireman named Paul Vickers and he worked reasonably well with Henry Eastburn, the resident engineer. Difficulties were found however in paying Vickers. In the 1790's the banking system was still in its infancy and monies paid to contractors by the company were normally handed over in cash. When work was taking place some distance from Lancaster this could be inconvenient and Gregson suggested to Vickers that he be paid by bank draft. This piece of paper would be sent from Gregson in Lancaster to Vickers who would then take it to a bank in Preston and draw the money needed to pay his workmens' wages. But this, protested Vickers, would be an inconvenience to him for a journey to Preston could take a considerable amount of time – especially if he was working on the southern part of his section. He did not seem keen on a bank draft either. Could not Gregson send money to Wigan, he asked, and could not the payment be made in cash? Eventually

Gregson worked out a compromise. If Vickers wanted cash then he should have it but sending cash to Wigan was too difficult for 'We cannot get the money conveyed to Wigan as no mail coach goes from hence to that place'. Instead the armed guard on the Mail Coach that called at both Lancaster and Chorley should be entrusted with the money. Vickers agreed to this plan and it seemed to have worked well with the contractor meeting the coach personally to take charge of the cash.

One thing which Vickers and Eastburn found worrying on their section of the canal, but which was not a problem in the north was the danger posed by old mine shafts. Many pits had been dug in the area through which the canal was to pass and if seams had been exhausted and closed there was a danger that the canal could be unwittingly dug slightly above a gallery that ran not too deep beneath the surface of the earth. If this eventually caused a collapse of the canal bed, water might pour through and flood other sections of a coal pit that was still in use. A company agent therefore walked about villages on the line asking old coal miners if they remembered any shafts that might cause such a failure.

The canal bed in fact stayed firm but the company did have problems with the masonry work done by their contractor Peter Grant. After an inspection of the line in 1794 a complaint was made by Gregson that 'very little is done and that little not at all well.' Later the walls of a small aqueduct built on the River Douglas began to bulge necessitating a fair amount of rebuilding and the company blamed this on Grant's poor supervision.

If the company were dissatisfied with the contractors however there were occasions when they in turn irritated their workpeople. The committee were always concerned with their public image. They wanted the works around Lancaster completed as soon as possible so as to impress visitors to the town and were not pleased when anything disturbed the image of the canal and its works as a wholly good thing. On one occasion Gregson wrote to Vickers

> *"I am sorry to be informed that some of your men have been behaving in a riotous and illegal manner at Chorley. Such conduct will bring disgrace upon the works, as well as upon yourselves."*

He then went on to urge Vickers to control his men more carefully and to help the authorities catch the ring leaders. In all probability Vickers could not have cared less what his men did when they were not working so long as it did not interfere with their ten hours and would have been hard put to do anything about it even had he wanted to. Moreover some notable men in society were not above using the riotous qualities of the diggers for their own ends either. 1796 was election year and Eastburn wrote:

"We are going very ill with work in this neighbourhood not a man has been at work since the canvassing began and I doubt it will be the case so long as the election continues. Lord Stanley's party having hired them, which can be for no other purpose than to riot and do mischief."

So long as Eastburn made no complaints the company were usually happy enough to let the contractors on the southern section get on with it. Eastburn's section was much smaller than that north of the Ribble, anyway, it was a long way from Lancaster and the committee, if not preoccupied with problems on the northern section tended to concentrate on the construction of that masterpiece of civil engineering the Lune Aqueduct.

5 The Lune Aqueduct

As Pinkerton and Murray's pick and shovel men toiled in the hills Rennie was making preparations for the construction of the Lune Aqueduct He must have been conscious of the fact that its failure could ruin his reputation, for nothing would have been worse than an arch collapsing into the Lune, cascading millions of gallons of water into the river, possibly causing loss of life and certainly a good deal of time and money. He therefore erred on the safe side in its design and planned an immensely strong construction based on the traditional technology of bridge building. There were to be 5 semi-circular arches rising some 50 feet from the water surface. Each span 70 feet and the total length of the aquaduct was to be 664 feet. The piers were to be supported by wooden piles driven into the riverbed. This was quite safe since wood, when permanently wet, does not rot. When the piles were in place their heads were to be covered by planks and then the masonry work was to be started on that. The piers were to be built hollow, of stone strengthened with iron bars and as these 'boxes' rose their centres were to be filled with rubble. A masonry arch is a structure which depends for its strength on wedge shaped stones which all lean on one another and are locked together by friction. Because an arch will not support itself unless all the stones are in position it has to be supported whilst being erected. Wooden scaffolding (called centering) was to be set into the Lune for this purpose therefore until the final keystone of each arch of the aqueduct was in place. Rennie went through the detailed planning with the constructing agent Alexander Stevens, he specified exactly how the building stones should be cut and dressed and how they should be put together. He gave detailed instructions on the length and thickness of the iron bars that he wanted to be used to reinforce the stonework and was very particular on the way in which mortar used to bond the stones was to be mixed. He wanted a special mortar mixing machine to be shipped from London and the committee agreed to this and it was ordered. He also wanted a substance called pozzalano to be mixed with lime and river sand to make a special mortar for that part of the aqueduct that would permanently be beneath the surface of the River Lune. This was more of a problem for the material had to be brought from Italy and since all British shipping was subject to attack by the French navy and privateers there was a danger that if the pozzalano ship sailed alone it might be captured and taken as a prize. The alternative however was a long wait in Leghorn (the Italian port from which the ship would sail) until enough England bound vessels came together to make a 'safety in numbers' convoy. The committee had to decide on this and in July of 1793 took the risk of authorising the ship to sail alone. In the event their decision was justified for the pozzalano arrived safely in Lancaster in the autumn of the same year.

When Stevens and Rennie had agreed eventually on how the aqueduct should be built preparations were made to start work on the river. Dredgers were used to scrape the bottom of the Lune at those points where the piers were to be built and then watertight walls had to be erected around the places on the riverbed where the work was to take place.

These walls were known as coffer dams and were constructed of thick wooden beams (known as sheeting piles) driven into the riverbed by men working from boats. No matter how well the coffer dam was built however water would seep in underneath and this would need to be pumped out. For this purpose Rennie had a steam engine ordered from the firm of Boulton and Watt in Birmingham.

A small engine house was built on the south bank of the Lune a few yards to the east of the proposed aquaduct so that when the steam engine was going it would drive, by a series of wooden beams, the pumps installed in the coffer dams. Though Stevens agreed to provide fuel for the steam engine it remained the property of the

company and they had to provide a man to look after it. For the piles themselves the company used mostly Russian timber, the sailing boat 'Nancy' being chartered to sail between Lancaster and the port of Memel in the Baltic Sea to bring it.

Work was started on the Lune Aqueduct much later than on the line but it was not long before Millar became as disillusioned with Stevens's foundation laying as he had been with Pinkerton and Murray's line cutting. He told the committee that the way in which Stevens was making the coffer dams would result in the steam engine being unable to pump out enough water to keep them from flooding. At this the committee acted quickly, they called for Stevens and told him that, although they were quite happy for him to do the masonry work when the foundations were completed they would not allow him to continue laying them. He had no option but to agree and Millar took complete charge. For the workmen on site this was a mixed blessing, for though Millar was a good company servant he had little regard for the ordinary worker and could be a hard taskmaster. All day and sometimes through the night the work went on, Millar soon having 200 men working in the coffer dams or on the bankside. When timber had been cut to size it was carried over a platform to a coffer dam and set ready for one of the pile engines to drive it into the riverbed. Those engines were all man powered and the labourers who used them certainly earned their two shillings a day. They were no more than simple wooden dereks with a pulley wheel in the centre. A heavy weight was attached to one end of a rope. This was then passed through the pulley wheel and men on the other end would then heave the weight into the air before letting it drop on the pile. The steam engine meanwhile kept up its steady rhythm pumping water day and night, its roaring fire consuming over a ton of fuel a day.

Unfortunately, this steady pace was all too often upset. Steam engines were still quite primitive and prone to failure. Parts broke because they were not designed to carry the load that was being put on them, and more durable replacements had to be made on the spot or sent away to Scottish iron-foundries for re-casting. The difficulties caused by the steam engines were not eased by troublesome engine attendants or firemen as they were called. One, James Law, stayed in bed one day and sent his mother to tell Millar that he would not return to work unless his wages were improved. On another occasion a new fireman stayed drunk for four days on the run. Drink was always a problem on the works, although it was quite normal for the company to provide free beer to the workmen.

In general Millar had little regard for many of the staff that the company employed and was not slow in making his feelings known. The company realised Millar's worth however and even took his side against the great John Rennie when there was a dispute between Pinkerton and Stevens over quarry stone. Gregson wrote to Rennie saying:

> *"We are sorry to observe you have contributed in some measure to give Stevens the wrong impression of Millar respecting the quarries. He never in the smallest degree counteracted any wishes of yours respecting them or indeed anything else, even where a difference prevailed he has been remarkably delicate and in every instance as far as we are able to judge has proved himself an active, steady and able agent."*

Being active, steady and able Millar regarded only those who were like minded with respect and was lucky in engaging an assistant engineer, William Cartwright who was as tough as himself. Once when the pile drivers discovered that Stevens's labourers were earning a few pence a day more than themselves they decided to

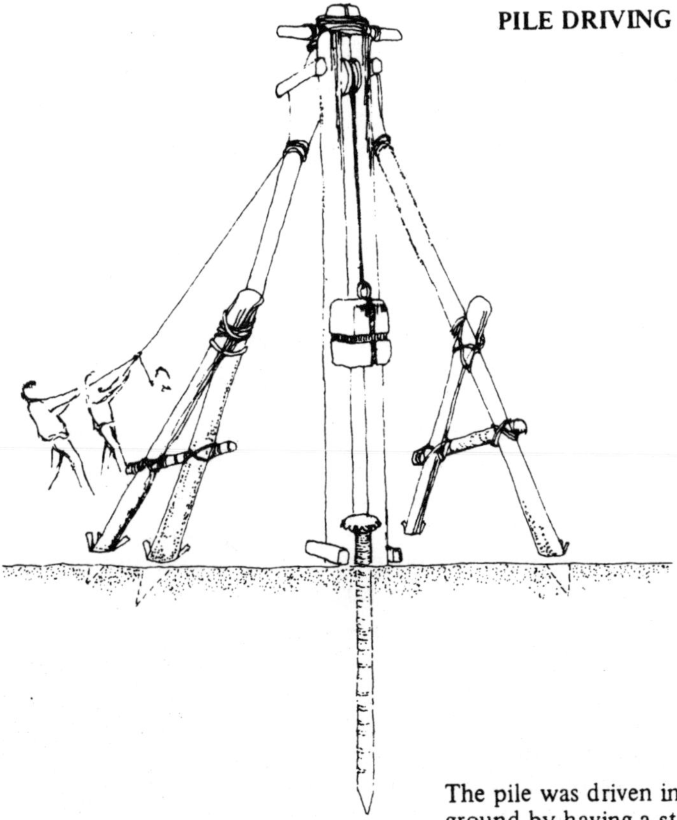

The pile was driven into the ground by having a stone or metal weight repeatedly dropped on it.

strike. There were no trade unions in those days so they made spontaneous 'combinations' and refused to work. 'These combinations', commented Millar, 'retard and are great evils'. He agreed with Cartwright that the company should sack the lot. All the men wanted was 14/- a week for six ten hour days and 3 pence an hour for overtime, but Millar wrote: 'Money, money, money is the common cry, I've heard nothing of work, work, work'. He also grumbled that the men would not work in the rain and wanted them to toil on Sundays. Treated like this it is hardly surprising that the labourers deserted the aqueduct works in the summer to take employment with local farmers on the harvest, but in the autumn they had to return.

Under Cartwright's direction the work went on apace through the winter and into the spring of 1795. As the foundations were completed Stevens's masons moved in and began the piers. Eventually when all the foundations and pier bases were completed the coffer dams were removed. The aqueduct was then raised arch by arch working from the south bank. A wooden platform was constructed so that stone, rubble and iron could be brought by cart to where it was needed and the arches of the piers themselves were supported by wooded scaffolding until ready to stand on their own. The company gave up its constructional responsibility for the aquaduct when the foundations were completed, they took down the steam engine and sold it and the pile drivers were dismissed. But as a token of the esteem in which they held Cartwright they set 17 guineas aside with which they purchased a silver cup and presented it to him as a reward for the extra care and attention he had shown in the construction of the Lune Aqueduct.

The aqueduct was completed in autumn of 1796 when a 3′ puddle was laid in its canal channel. It was then connected to the south bank of the Lune with another substantial piece of engineering, an embankment that ran into Lancaster.

This embankment had been the source of some anxiety to the committee during the time of Pinkerton and Murray's work and afterwards. It was huge and required an enormous amount of earth to complete, much of which had to be dug by hand at Ashton Hill. At first the company built special carts to carry the earth, but when the Ashton Hill to Lancaster section of the canal was completed Pinkerton suggested that boxes, about 1 yard square, be used, which could be filled with earth and then removed on rollers to a flat boat moored on the canal. When the deck of this was filled with such boxes it was taken off to Lancaster. When the end of the waterway was reached the boxes would be unloaded, tipped over and then, empty, sent back to Ashton Hill. Thus would hundreds of tons of earth be moved.

When the finishing touches were being put to the Lune Aqueduct, and the last earth being thrown on the embankment then one man who might have breathed a sigh of relief deeper than most others was Samuel Gregson. For Millar the end of the contract meant the sack but for Gregson hopefully many fruitful years as the secretary of a successful canal company. The past four years had been very trying for, whenever there was trouble either with landowners or the contractors Gregson had been deep in the fray. One day for example he had to go to Whittle to discuss compensation for damage that had been done by the canal workers with a Mr. Heatley. Mr. Heatley demanded that payment be made at once and when Gregson said he could not do that Mr. Heatley became very angry. He called Gregson and all the committee members thieves. He said they had squandered the subscribers' money and now wanted to plunder and steal the land of honest men, his language said Gregson was 'too gross and insulting to bear'. But bear it he did and kept his temper too although he found the matter very depressing and admitted to being down in the dumps as a result.

6 Completion

Argument of the kind that took place between Mr. Heatley and Samuel Gregson took place against a background of a long struggle with the Leeds and Liverpool Canal Company, worries over not having enough money to pay for the completion of the canal and unrest amongst some of the shareholders. The Leeds and Liverpool Company had not quite decided how they would complete their canal to Liverpool when work on the Lancaster started and Gregson and his associates were amazed when they found out that the Leeds and Liverpool committee wanted to build their line almost parallel to the Lancaster Canal! Arguments (and insults) grew as the months passed until eventually it was agreed that the Leeds and Liverpool would be joined to the Lancaster at Johnsons Hillock and near Wigan. Suddenly all was well and the two companies became the best of friends.

Many problems were not so easily solved. As the wars with the French, that had begun in 1792, continued, prices began to rise and people found that their money did not go quite so far as before. Also they saw that a number of canals begun at the same time as the Lancaster had failed and that subscribers to them had lost all their money. Worried by this they became slower at paying their calls and so Gregson and Worswick found themselves having to pay more for the things needed by the canal company whilst having money coming in at a slower rate.

Then there were unpleasant noises from the direction of Kendal where merchants saw no sign of the canal being extended past Tewitfield and wanted to know what was going on. Gregson and some committee members had to go to Kendal in December of 1796 to assure everybody that things would go as quickly as possible but that number one priority was getting the Preston to Lancaster line open. He told them that he hoped that this would be completed in the following summer and sure enough it was later announced that the canal would be officially opened on November 22nd, 1797.

The official opening of the Lancaster Canal was a splendid affair. Six boats left Lancaster to sail up to the aqueduct In them were the canal committee and their friends, a few shareholders and local celebrities. Red coated guardsmen provided an escort and a battery of artillery on the Moor sounded a salute as the flotilla got underway. After viewing the aqueduct the little convoy, now with a boat containing limestone in tow, made its way to Galgate. Here the limestone was exchanged for coal that had been brought up from Preston, so making a gesture to trade which, it was hoped would soon flourish.

But the celebration that marked the opening of the Tewitfield to Preston section did not hide the fact that the company had two canals, one of which had yet to be completed and the other which was completely cut off from the main canal network. The committee now applied itself to getting traffic going on both sections and making plans for a connection between the north and south ends. On the north end attempts were made to encourage the limestone trade and the construction of lime kilns at Borwick and Preston but trade was slow to pick up and so Gregson and some committee members began to trade on the canal themselves. When they came to apply themselves to the problem of the Ribble crossing they found that some people thought that Rennie's aqueduct would now cost far too much to build. By 1800 William Cartwright had become resident engineer of the company and he said that a far better idea would be to build a wooden bridge over the river and then have a tramway linking the southern terminal of the north end with the northern terminal of the south end. The committee asked Rennie his opinion and their first engineer agreed that

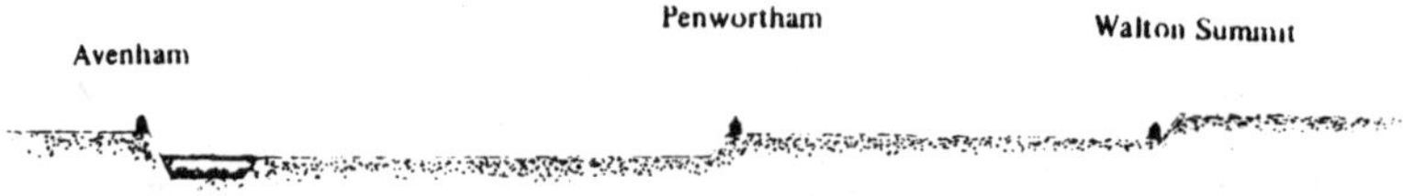

The waggons were drawn up the inclines by steam engines. The one at Avenham was typical. It was of six horsepower and made by a firm named Wilkinson which was based in Wrexham. On the insistance of a local landowner it was constructed so that it would consume its own smoke. All the engines were housed in sheds. At Avenham and Penwortham these sheds were at the top of the inclines, at Walton Summit at the bottom.

THE RAILWAY CONNECTION
(Not to Scale)

Cartwright's idea was sound but that in the longer term, an aqueduct as originally planned would be far better.

The committee decided to build the tramway however and under Cartwright's supervision work began between the Preston Basin and Johnsons Hillock. The south end of the canal was extended northwards to Walton Summit whilst the track and bridge works were prepared. There were to be two tracks, used by waggons going in different directions. The one used by waggons going north was called the coal or descending road and the one used by south bound waggons called the limestone or ascending road. The tracks were made of cast iron rails mounted on stone blocks that were shipped in from Lancaster. Cartwright was not pleased with the first lot of rails that arrived from Scotland, he found them so roughly made and brittle that he sent them back and ordered a new lot, this time from an English Iron foundry.

The link was completed in 1804 and was very successful in increasing the trade between the two sections of the Lancaster Canal. Most of the tramway was level but there were three points on the track (at Avenham, Penwortham and Walton Summit) where there were very steep inclines and for these the company made special provision. At each of these inclines a small engine shed was built to house a stationary steam engine that drove an endless chain. When a train of tram waggons arrived to go to a higher level they could be connected to a link in the chain and as the chain began to move so it would pull the waggons upwards. If waggons arrived to go downwards then linking them to the chain would also assist with braking.

To go from Preston to Walton Summit would mean one descent and two ascents and to come back two descents and one ascent with freight being transhipped at either end between waggon and barge. It was a much more costly and time consuming operation than simply hauling a boat across an aquaduct but as far as the company was concerned the best short term solution to a difficult problem.

Ingenious and successful a device as the tram link was it soon became by far the most dangerous part of the canal due to the number of accidents caused by the sudden snapping of a link in the endless chain. Horses were often left in harness on the inclines and their attendants (although they were not allowed to) sometimes rode on the waggons. If the chain broke then the waggons would plunge downhill dragging the unfortunate men and beasts with them – sometimes to an unpleasant death. The company tried to improve matters with rules about waggon load weight but the accidents continued, probably due more to the state of metal technology than to overloading.

But accidents or not when the link between the northern and southern sections of the canal was finally completed, the result for company finance was good and immediate, the income from tollage nearly doubling. Now the only major work to be completed was the Tewitfield to Kendal section.

The traders of Kendal became more and more irritated as the years went by and nothing was done to bring the canal to their town and they were not the only ones displeased with the company in its first few years of operation. Although Gregson had entered trade on the canal when it was first opened because few others showed interest some traders who came to use the canal later thought that he had become too wealthy on the profits and suggested that he was using his position as clerk to the company to make himself richer still. Why, they asked, did a coal company in which Gregson was a partner, supply coal to the Ribble Bridge Steam Engine? His coal was not the cheapest and there were others who would willingly supply it at a lower price. Why did Gregson have to have an assistant, surely he did not have so much work to do now as before and was it not strange that this assistant just happened to be Gregson's son? To investigate these and other charges against Gregson a special committee was set up. The people who had made the charges against Gregson were pleased at that, but certainly not at the fact that many of the people who were on it seemed to be friends of associates of his. The committee of inquiry certainly gave a report which was very favourably inclined towards Gregson, dismissing all the charges and saying that there had not even been one 'self interested, partial or obvious transaction'. Pleased or not the complainants could do little further although Gregson did agree to stop trading on the canal for so long as he remained company secretary.

Was Gregson guilty of making a profit out of the company? It is hard to tell really, but without Gregson's spirit and energy there may never have been a Lancaster Canal to trade on anyway. Other members of the canal committee certainly had their own business expanded by the canal. John Brockbank for instance supplied timber for use on the Lune Aqueduct and for making waggons, a number of canal boats were built in his shipyard and he was a partner in the company that supplied coal to the Ribble Bridge stationary engine.

What Kendal men thought of the arguments is anybody's guess though they probably would have welcomed Gregson or anyone else working on the canal – if they had one. It was not until 1817 that work started between Tewitfield and Kendal however and the work brought the troubles of rampaging navvies back to the countryside.

The new line extension was 14½ miles long and the major engineering works were eight locks at Tewitfield, the 378 yard long Hincaster Tunnel and a reservoir at Killington. The Hincaster Tunnel was built to take the canal close to the gunpowder works at Sedgwick and the product of that place possibly assisted the tunnellers in their work. When the rock and earth had been removed then the bricklayers moved in to line the tunnel with bricks. Unfortunately what they did not do was to build a towpath and so

the boatmen had to pull their vessels through by a rope that ran along the tunnel side. The canal tunnel was completed by Christmas Day 1817 but it was not until the summer of 1819 that a grand opening ceremony was held in Kendal to celebrate its completion. During that time the corporation of Kendal had constructed a canal basin with wharves and warehouses ready for the days when boats would sail to Kendal. When they did it made more difference to that town than to any other on the canal and one writer pointed out that Kendal 'assumed a new and modern approach. So very different that any person having been absent for a few years could scarcely have identified it'.

With the construction of the Kendal branch the main line of the canal was complete. The Glasson Dock branch was built a few years later and this allowed small coastal sailing ships to go right up to Kendal or down to Preston. The canal never reached Westhoughton though, nor was an aqueduct ever built over the Ribble, so the north remained as it remains still, isolated from the main canal network.

From start to finish the Lancaster Canal and its branches took thirty three years to build. In the end did the waterway fulfil men's hopes? For the merchants of Lancaster who had anticipated that it would enable their town to compete on a firm footing with Liverpool we must say no – though not due so much to any failing of the canal itself as to the relative decline of Lancaster as a port. There were a number of reasons for this. The wars were a major problem. Increasing attacks by French privateers obliged the British Government to order all but the best armed ships coming from the West Indies to sail in convoy. Unfortunately this meant that all ships coming from the Caribbean arrived at once and this caused a glut of West Indian produce on the market. Prices therefore fell and Lancaster merchants soon found themselves having a hard time. The wars dragged on until 1815 by which time Liverpool was firmly established as England's major port. It had everything; good docks, short lines of communication to the heartland of industrial England, financial know how and go ahead merchants. Lancaster simply could not compete with it in any serious way even with Glasson Dock and the Lancaster Canal.

But other men prospered as a result of the canal even if some Lancaster merchants did not. Those who dealt in lime and coal for example and the merchants of Kendal. The farmer got his cheap fertilizer so he could make his land richer and the poor man his cheap coal so he could keep his house warmer. John Brockbank prospered as did Samuel Gregson. People who subscribed to the canal saw a fair return on their money – even if it was not as high as some had hoped.

But what of the wandering canal worker who had picked and puddled, carted and carried? Well on the pay roll of the company at the time of the building of the Lune Aqueduct was one John Rose, pile driver. Over fifty years later he wrote to the company from the Preston workhouse. His letter read:

Gentlemen,

With humble confidence I take the liberty of troubling you, hoping you will look upon me as one superannuated and consequently almost destitute of old friends, having out lived most of my old patrons. Several gentlemen in Preston have advised me to write to Mr. Gregson for they say they are sure he would do something for me, as here we have no chance of getting a penny towards a little tobacco but what an old friend may sometimes give us. It is my desire with your aprobation that you let Mr. Gregson see this letter, hoping he will not be offended with the liberty I am taking with him, my small sum would be acknowledge by me with heart felt gratitude.

I am your humble servant,
John Rose

I wonder if he got his money?